Likes Don't Pay Bills

How to Leverage Social Media to Get Leads and Customers

By: Chris Oberg

Table of Contents

Introduction

Your customers are on social media. They are probably scrolling their feeds right now, as you are reading this. How can I know that? Because *everyone's* customers are on social media all the time.

With the right strategies, you can get their attention, connect with them, and build relationships with them. However, with the wrong strategies, they will scroll right past your posts, and your attempt to use social media as a marketing tool can be a frustrating time-sink.

This book will discuss the many strategies involved in using social media to get leads, customers, and sales. The first part of the book talks about the five biggest myths surrounding social media marketing and what to do instead. The second part of the book teaches you copywriting and email marketing, which are essential skills in the online marketing world.

After you have read this book, you will have all you need to leverage social media to build your platform and get tons of warm leads and turn them into customers for life.

Let's jump right in and start with social media marketing myth #1!

Part 1 – Five Social Media Marketing Myths

Myth 1:
Your Followers Care about You

As the number of followers increases, it is easy to get caught up and think that they really care about you. They like your posts after all. This illusion that just because someone hits "like" on your post, they actually like *you* can be very dangerous to some.

Imagine a teenage girl posting makeup tips. The more likes and shares that she has, the more she may believe in the value of the system itself. She may even associate her own value and worth on the number of likes. Do the people who watch her videos actually care about her as a person? Unfortunately, probably not.

The truth is that most followers don't care about you or your posts. It just so happens that your post came across in their feed as they scroll catatonically through countless other posts, ads, and messages.

Although many people are using social media to promote a business or bring awareness to something, there are others who just post for the sake of posting. Do you think that their followers actually care about them? Did they stir some type of emotion in the followers?

So, if we know that your followers do not naturally care about you, the question is how do we make them care? It does sound fairly easy but consider how do we get people to actually care about us in the real world? How do you create an emotional bond with someone with whom you seemingly have nothing in common with?

Sending a Message to Your Followers

Let's start with the basics. What does it really mean for people to care about you? By definition, the word caring means to display kindness and concern for others. It is showing empathy and feelings of compassion for another person. It is touching a person in an emotional way that makes them want to or be willing to inconvenience themselves for your benefit.

We all meet random people every day. But there is no emotional bond established with each and every one of these. There is no possible way for a celebrity like Selena Gomez to have an emotional connection with each and every one of the 100+ million followers through daily, regular, generic posts.

However, if your message is able to meet a person where they are at, touching him or her through your words, pictures and actions, you will be able to create that bond and emotional connection. You have to hit them deep. Reach them in a way that they never expected. Communicate your message in such a way as to express your understanding of their hopes, fears and dreams. Allow them to use their imagination about your relationship and define it as if it is real.

If you are creating posts and messages that appeal to YOU as if you are the audience, then you probably have misread who your audience is and what they really want. Do your research. Determine who it is that you are speaking to, who you want to reach and what is it that they are hoping to receive from you. This is where the value in your message will lie. Take the extra time to research, use the vocabulary of those you are speaking to. Address the real pain points and in fact, be real!

Going back to the celebrities who have a large following. Each of them shares their real stories, and their real struggles with those who want to know. Selena Gomez for example shares her personal struggles with relationships and her career. She engages her followers and lets them know that she understands their struggles too. She shares that her success has come after trials and hardships. She is not simply posting random pictures and posts about unnecessary topics.

Let your audience project their own fantasies towards your message as well.

Learning What Makes People Tick

Great marketing is mostly about learning exactly what people care about: what makes them tick. We know that people do not really care about you when they are looking up to your service. They care about themselves, and how you may help them solve a certain problem. But in most cases, there is more to that.

People will say all kinds of nice things – but in most cases, it is all a façade. Nowadays, the average customer is well-researched, and, likely, they have already gone through countless of your competitors before they got up to you. This is why they will analyze you based on various other circumstances. The trick here is to figure out exactly what makes them tick – what they care about. Here is how you can figure that out:

Identify Their Problems

When you sell a product to a client, you are not selling them a product that you just want to bring into the world: you sell a product that you believe will make their lives easier. You can't sell a customer a product unless it improves their life – it's impractical, yet many business owners put themselves into this situation.

To find out what makes your audience tick, you need to understand who they are – and specifically, what pains they have. Your purpose here is to create a product that may alleviate that pain. Otherwise, you won't be able to get your business going.

Many small business owners are struggling to get out in the world by creating a product, and then present it to a wide audience, hoping that they can attract the right people – but in the meantime, they end up forgetting who their audience is. They are so focused on attracting potential customers that they no longer remember who they are trying to reach. They don't have their pains in mind – but a general product that might solve a certain widespread problem.

This is why, in order to connect with your audience, you need to go to the places that they currently are – no matter if it's in a physical place or a social media one. Try to talk to them regularly and learn about any problems that they might have. Look at reviews and complaints about similar products – see what their actual desires are. This way, you can create better products that you may launch at the right audience.

Mind the Vocabulary

Your followers do not particularly care about you. In fact, they just care about what you say, and how your words are resonating with whatever they have in mind. They care about the way you speak, how your words connect to them.

Whenever you are speaking, not only do you have to be clear in the words that you are using, but you should also use a language that seems attractive to them. A lawyer will not attract potential customers by using the "ghetto language" – they will want to seem as professional as possible. In this case, they might want to use a few "fancy" words that will help deliver an image.

At the same time, if your audience is formed out of people such as students or stay-at-home mothers, then you might want to refrain from the extra professional language. Your fancy, pompous words will not phase them in the way that you are hoping – and in truth, it might just send them in a different direction. People are looking for the kind of language and behavior that they can connect to, not the kind that will ascertain your show-off qualities.

Bear in mind that your vocabulary should also contain "trigger words" – or as marketers refer to them, "words that sell." Certain words in your vocabulary may attract customers to your side, keeping them there with certain words that sell. They may not realize it themselves, but words such as "you," "new," or even something as simple as "tips" may earn you quite a few followers. This is because you can manage to connect to them on a deeper level – as long as you also learn how to steer clear of clichés.

The same thing goes with the vocabulary that your potential customer is using. What words are they using? Do they seem like they are trying to convey something to you? What words are they using specifically – and do they mostly consist of positive or negative words? Do they seem to be using a lot of "mhm" words or short monosyllabic responses? If that is the case, even if they are your followers or not, it is likely that you will not be able to hang on to them for very long.

By lending an ear at the words that your potential customers are using, you will be able to figure out exactly what makes them tick. What do they seem to be interested in? What exactly does it seem particularly boring to them? The richer their vocabulary, the more they might be interested in what you have to sell them. Your tone of voice will also be quite determinant, as they will be looking for someone with a calm attitude – not someone that will rush them into taking action.

Pay Attention to the Body Language

When you are talking with a customer, you should pay attention to your body language and the body language of your client. Specifically, you might want to focus on the feedback that your customer is giving you – although this mostly applies to when you are speaking with the customer face to face.

Most of the advice that we receive in concerns to feedback focuses on the things that we have to say – but the non-verbal communication is very important as well. For example, by conveying discomfort or aggression using your body language, you might end up making them feel unsafe – therefore, preventing them from further listening to what you have to say. Sometimes, it's the little gestures that give away the way they feel – and all you have to do is "listen" to what their body language is telling you. If they do not feel a connection to what you are trying to convey to them through your body language, then you might just lose them in the long run.

Myth 2:
More Likes and Shares are Better

We all love that feeling when you post something on Facebook or Instagram and you watch the number of LIKES go up. You feel accomplished as the volume of shares increases by the minute and you know that more and more people are viewing your message. We tend to feel better about ourselves and the message we are trying to spread as we watch the likes and shares increase.

We want the message to go viral, thinking that will increase our popularity and in turn, our money. The myth that the more likes that you have the more famous or rich you will be is simply that, a myth and will hurt your opportunities to truly be famous or rich if you let it.

In reality, likes won't pay your bills or put food on the table. The algorithms that sites like Facebook and Instagram utilize will certainly spread your message far and wide, but for what purpose. Is the number of likes truly an indicator of the success of your social media marketing?

The Marketing Measurements

As it is said, what gets measured gets done. In the case of social media marketing, what gets measured, gets

the attention. The number of likes simply shows the popularity of the fan page. It does not necessarily indicate that the follower will go out and purchase the product. It displays brand awareness and knowledge. Or simply that the particular ad was attractive or appealing.

At the end of 2017, Buffer.com conducted a study of posts, which were the highest ranking for the year. A post by a photographer who had created a warped view of the world reached more than 803,000 people, was shared 2,300 times and reacted to more than 9K times. However, it did not earn any money. It was simply an engagement post. Kudos to the person who posted it for these very impressive numbers but unfortunately, it did not make this photographer a millionaire.

Another post, about Instagram marketing, received 644 reactions, reached more than 334,000 people and most importantly, was clicked on 34, 372 times. This last number is an indication that not only did viewers see the ad, but it was of interest to them and they wanted to learn more. This emotional response triggered an action. The advertiser struck a nerve, prompting more than 34K people to follow the link and engage.

This reaction, prompting an action is the key to your social media marketing. It is not the advertisement itself that will bring in the revenue, but instead the emotional response that you will incite in your potential client. That emotion, feeling or interest is what will prompt them to take action.

Consider the infamous commercials during the Half Time Show at the Super Bowl. People everywhere are at parties, the local bar or on the couch waiting with baited breath to see what the creative will put out there for your viewing pleasure. In the coffee room the next morning, the conversation typically revolves around the best and of course, worst commercials. The discussion probably swirls around the commercials even more so than the game itself. It would be an interesting study to review and evaluate the conversation surrounding both the best and worst to see which product is actually identified with each commercial. I would be willing to bet that most people could not tell you. Although they LIKED the funny commercial with the old guy, they have no idea what product it was for. The heart-wrenching ad with the kittens may have tugged at your heartstrings, but will it make you immediately go out to buy whatever it is they are selling? Probably not.

As you can see, just because someone LIKES or even shares your post or your ad, you are simply generating awareness. A person is acknowledging in a way that he/she SAW it but then quickly moves on to the next one in the news feed. Imagine scrolling down through your posts and just hitting LIKE for each and every one. Did you actually read everyone's posts? Do you understand the message that each of your friend's was trying to share? What if they asked you about it later, could you tell them what it said? Probably not. You simply acknowledged that they were active on the site

and kept moving. Don't forget, there are a lot of posts to read!

The bottom line is this...is the number of likes really the best measurement of a successful post or campaign? A better way to measure is to evaluate what type of chain reaction you can begin with your posts. How many people have shared your message or talked about it with others?

Don't try to be all things to all people. Some entrepreneurs and business owners try to connect with and cater to all people. This strategy, not really a strategy at all, will diminish the value of your product and the market that you should be targeting to.

Draw a line in the sand. Figure out who in fact you should be targeting to and make a stand. Research the actual likes and dislikes of this demographic of people and focus your marketing strategy on providing them with the appropriate material to solicit an emotional response.

How will this impact you and your business you may be asking? By targeting those people with whom you can connect, you have a much better chance of them converting to an actual customer rather than simply clicking LIKE. This deceptive number or perception of popularity is still necessary but to truly gauge the value of your marketing, the number of sales that occurred as a result of your campaign is a much better measure.

Likes are the end result of a temporary feeling about your campaign. To successfully impact change and long-term sales and customers, you must focus of creating a strategy and content that will stand the test of time. In your efforts, you are looking to develop a brand that will be recognizable, memorable and longstanding.

I am sure you are familiar with many brands that have been able to endure throughout the years, amidst competition, varying promotional strategies and even challenges within the company itself. Companies like Levi Strauss, Colgate-Palmolive, Mercedes-Benz, Kraft, The New York Times and Tiffany & Co. have not only been able to endure and survive but actually come out on top.

Although times have changed and in fact, the markets may have changed, each of these companies has researched the target audience and tailored their marketing campaigns towards specific individuals with specific qualities and needs. This strategy has been used no matter whether the campaign was in print, billboard, or social media.

Just because Mercedes-Benz may have placed an amazing, historic commercial on the Super Bowl one year, and it was the topic of conversation the next day, that does not mean that the intended audience was EVERYONE who was watching at the time. The campaign was geared towards a certain type of person watching the game at the time; only that engagement will turn into a sale. It wasn't that the commercial was talked about or LIKED that made it an effective campaign. It was instead the number of people who felt a deeper connection with the message in the commercial; those who now felt that their desires, dreams and emotions were engaged and connected to are the ones who went out and in fact, purchased a Mercedes-Benz.

How will you engage your target audience?

Quality vs. Quantity – How to Make Sure You Get Quality

Some people focus a lot on the quantity of the product rather than on the quality. "The more, the merrier" – or this is how the saying generally goes. The problem is that if you wish for your marketing to be successful, you may want to focus on quality instead – because this is what matters.

In truth, both quality and quantity are important – buy you will need to create the right balance for both of them. For instance, let's say that you create a lot of posts every week, and you have quite a number of followers that like or share your product – but no one really buys it. So, while the product may seem to have potential, you haven't gone high enough to get profit.

On the other hand, if you create good quality content, it will be much easier for the followers to connect with what you have to say. Once they get engaged in your high-quality content, there is a high chance that this will also result in conversion. The more they stay on your website, the higher the chances are that they will buy something – and this can only happen if you create content that is attractive for the visitors.

The Question of "What to Measure"

So, what should you measure instead, if quantity is not something that you should put your trust in? Most people measure the likes that you get on a post – and in a way, it's good – because it gives you a good idea of how many people are interacting with your website.

But hear this: not every person that hits "like" on your post will access the link to your article/page. A lot of people will see the title, possibly agree with it, and then hit the like button as a reflex. Some may even access your post – but once they see that the quality of your post is not enough to keep them interested, they will hit "back" on that website as soon as they entered it. This will not help your website traffic much – in fact, it will only bring it down.

To make potential followers stick to your website, you need to create content that they will enjoy reading – that will give them enough reason to stay on your website for as long as it is needed to go through anything. The more they stay there, the higher the chances will be that search engines will pick on to this – deeming you as a quality website and putting you higher up the ranks.

The purpose of your post is not to get likes; everyone can get those. Nowadays, you can simply purchase those likes off the Internet – through accounts that deliver those likes to you. You can get the likes, which will make your post seem more popular – but in truth, there won't be many conversions for you there. You will need people to come in contact with your website – to get you the traffic that you deserve.

This is why instead of focusing on the likes that you get, you should focus on the traffic that your website receives. How many visitors do you get on your website on a daily basis? How much time do those people spend on your website? Do they stay there for only a few seconds, or do they spend more than a couple of minutes doing research? If they end up spending quite a lot of time there, then it's clear that your content brings them quite a lot of good information.

With each post, you are hoping to get new readers – readers that can benefit from your information. You want to help them make the right choice and inform them about the purchases that they want to make – give them all the details so that in the end, they pick you. This is why it does not make sense to focus on the likes when you need to keep them on board.

Your goal here is to measure the traffic and improve it if it's not working how you are hoping. Remember, your goal here is to get your traffic and obtain conversion – which is why you should spend less attention on the likes and more on the actual traffic.

Myth 3:
There Is So Much Noise, I Need to Find the Best Hack to Break Through

Noise, or things that are a distraction or not useful to you, are plentiful on social media. You are constantly hit with spam, junk email, ads for things you never knew you had searched for or even needed and even those cute little puppies. Your inbox is full of useless content and your feed is clogged with distractions.

Most people try to develop tactics to break through the noise and there are various things that have been tried. One strategy is to trick people into action. Unfortunately, this is a shortsighted strategy that focuses only on something you cannot control – those things that show up in feeds.

Instead of trying to trick people into clicking, your strategy should focus on connecting with people and bringing the discussion outside of social media. Yes. I said it. The horror! In our highly digital, technology driven world, most people cannot live a minute without their phone in their hand. They go to sleep scrolling and swiping right or left. They wake up to the alarm on their phone and before even setting foot out of the bed, they have checked email and Facebook for any new information.

The connection that you want to create to sidestep this concept of noise is to initiate a conversation online but have it continue outside of the virtual space – in the real world! You want people to be talking about it, sharing it, and yes, even dancing to it. Just like the wildly popular Gangnam Style.

Released in 2012, it became the first video on YouTube to hit 2 BILLION views. Yes, that's right! We are talking billions here! Not only were followers watching this soon to be famous video, but they were in fact sharing, liking and DOING the Gangnam style dance moves. Soon after, the artist, Psy, was accused of stealing some of his dance moves from another artist, causing controversy and of course, more discussion. Now everyone wanted to not only watch this Korean guy dance and sing, they wanted to compare it to another group's moves. The more discussion, the more traffic to the website, the more views and shares.

How does this translate to earnings? Although viewers watch videos on YouTube for free, the advertising that is displayed on the page is the revenue generator. As more and more people watched this amazing video, the more people who would see the ads, click and ultimately purchase something. According to Google's Chief Business officer, Psy's video brought in more than $8 million strictly through viewers on YouTube.

It was not a matter of how many followers Psy had or even how many people actually like him or his style. It was the conversations, the controversy and the fact that everyone needed to see what the hype was all about that drew the traffic to his video. He was able to break through the noise to create a winning product. Psy was not just another guy on the internet sharing his music. Between July and September of 2012, through word of mouth, Gangnam Style very quickly ascended the ranks of top videos and in this short time, had been viewed more than 2 million times. As the dance began to catch on, people began to record themselves dancing the Gangnam Style and posting on YouTube. This brought in additional views for Psy as viewers compared their dance to the original.

As the video began to go viral, it caught the attention of the media. Rather than Psy having to approach the media about his video to promote it and drive traffic, they were coming to HIM. The more press he received, the more traffic was driven to his video. What a truly amazing marketing campaign in which he really did not have to do much. What he did do was start a conversation in the social media landscape, which led to conversations *outside* social media. Through his music, he targeted a very specific group of people who he knew would want to listen to new, fresh music and would easily share and talk about his work.

This is how Psy broke through the noise and how you can too. It will require research and effort but, in the end, you will reap the benefits by having your products or services talked about outside of social media.

Of course, the first thing that you must do is identify your target market. Who are you selling to? What product or service will solve a problem that this particular group is interested in? Do your research and learn all that you can about this market.

Whether you start out with a following 100 or 1,000, you need to actively listen to what your audience is telling you; what do they like; what topics are regularly discussed. Utilize analytics to determine what it is they are talking about, what they react to and what posts and topics get the most attention. Listening is the first step towards writing great content that will stir a reaction in your intended audience. This emotional reaction will be the trigger for them to begin the conversation.

Through your content, you want to make your audience believe that they are important to you. Be relatable and transparent. You are not trying to trick anyone into buying or sharing information. Be your genuine self both on and offline by sharing your desire to help, influence or provide them with a benefit. When you speak to and connect with people on a level that is personal and non-salesy, you conquer the noise and develop an unbreakable bond.

In the marketing of Gangnam Style, we can only imagine what Psy's strategy was to market to his audience. His passion for music was evident in the video through his facial expressions and dance moves and he shared his love with his audience. This came through as a feel-good reaction which viewers just felt compelled to share with others. He connected with his audience on a deeper level than simply a new, upbeat song. He caused that emotional reaction that you should also be trying to obtain from you viewers, willing them to share it with others.

By getting to know your target audience, you can create great content about things that are important to them and about things that will help them create a better life. Pictures also speak a thousand words. When considering what will touch a person emotionally and will spark that further discussion, consider what visually sparks your interest. What pictures on Instagram make you pause your scrolling to look more carefully at it? What images take your breath away and then encourage you to show it to a friend or family member? Maybe it stirs an emotion that prompts a discussion.

This same emotion that is stirred within you is what you want to bring out for your followers. You want to use photos that will not only speak a thousand words to them but that they will in turn, speak a thousand words about. Your audience is the best promotion that you could ask for when the conversation is taken out of social media and into the real world. Inevitably, those that they talk about it with will come back to social media to see it for themselves or to join the online conversation.

Through your outstanding message and content, you can take a small group of diligent and faithful followers and turn them into your marketing army. By consistently sharing the same message, you establish yourself as reliable, trustworthy and knowledgeable. People will see you as someone who cares about their needs which will in turn, build your reputation and encourage them to discuss and share.

Consider the local motivational speaker who regularly posts inspirational and motivational content. He knows what it is that his followers want and what they react to. His content continuously creates an emotional response within each and every person that it touches. His message is shared countless numbers of times on social media and discussed between friends. New followers seek out his websites to hear his inspiring words for themselves. His message is no longer simply another of the many inspiring messages that pass through the news feed, adding to the social media noise. They have instead become sought after, daily nuggets of affirmation. Each and every follower feels the connection with the speaker as if they are personal friends, and the valuable feelings that go with it.

Myth 4:
Post X Times per Day at Exactly X O'clock

I have to post every day at the same time to ensure that my audience is available and ready to receive my message. NOT!

When it comes to social media marketing, we tend to focus on how many times per day and what time we post. This strategy assumes that people only check their social media feeds at certain times and does not take into account the other more important factors.

If you have done your research, you will already understand that when people are interested in a particular topic, they will follow and view your content. By connecting with your small group of followers, your targeted audience, you can be assured that they will see it. They want to see it and if you are being consistent, with powerful and fulfilling content, they will seek it out no matter what time of day or what day of the week you post it.

Studies of trends in social media originally suggested that to reach the maximum number of followers and to increase your engagement, you had to post during commuting time, lunch and break times, and evenings. This slightly outdated information has not been updated with new trends and to cover unique target groups.

Rather than focusing on the specific times and days that you should be posting, instead focus on what works best for YOUR followers. By having an understanding of the habits and social media routines of your audience, you can better determine what will be the best time to post to gain the most exposure for your content.

The key here is for YOUR content. Each target market or audience will have its own best time to post. For example, if you are targeting moms of young children, you can be pretty sure that rush hour and mid-afternoon will NOT be appropriate times to post content. They will be too busy getting kids on and off the bus or to and from school to notice your post. However, if you post at 9pm, you might be more likely to get their attention after the children are settled in for the night and finally get some "me" time to scroll through social media. It may even be their guilty pleasure for the day, the only time they have to read something that interests them. Because this may be a similar time for others as well, they may not only see it, but share it and then chat about it at tomorrow's PTA meeting since it will be fresh in their minds.

On the other hand, if you are promoting a new deli that has just opened up in town, you may want to post and share mouth-watering pictures of the delicacies that you offer at 11am each day. You can be pretty sure that people will be searching for lunch options around this time and what better time to engage not only their senses but their stomachs as well. If they then come in to purchase lunch from your deli, you can now establish a deeper connection in person, encouraging them to start a conversation off of social media as well with others to stop in and enjoy your food.

When it comes to social media, of course, your goal should be to gain the most engagement within the first few hours of posting. Studies have shown that the likelihood of your post being seen decreases as the time goes on. Going back to the deli, it would not be a good idea to post about your new lunch specials AFTER the lunch rush. At that point, you would simply be adding to the social media noise as your followers scroll past your post on their way to find something else that interests them.

Have you ever heard your friend say "did you see Jane's post last week?" Unless you saw it shortly after Jane posted it, it is highly possible that the noise in your social media feed has overpowered Jane's post and it is no longer visible or even relevant any longer. That being said, you need to capitalize on the momentum of engagement and not only post but engage with your audience while they are available.

If you recall, earlier in this book we discussed proactively connecting with and reactively connecting with your audience. By interacting with them during this time after you post, you are reinforcing your concern for them and their importance to you. As you receive comments on your posts, be sure to respond as soon as possible.

However, we have also seen that trends have changed as many people pick up their phones to mindlessly scroll through their social media feeds before they even set foot out of bed. So, in reality, no matter what time of day, or how many times you post, either your followers will see it or they won't. There is no perfect time or pre-determined number of times per week that contains the magic number to guarantee that followers will see it and engage.

Instead, focus on producing great content and posting regularly, whatever that means to you. Maybe it is once per day or once per week, but create a regular schedule of posting so that your followers will look forward to receiving your engaging content at that particular time. By consistently posting amazing content, you will automatically draw people in as loyal followers who are willing to share and discuss with their friends.

Another problem with social media posting is the actual algorithms that are behind the scenes running the show. Have you ever wondered how it is that they know that you recently searched for a place to take a new yoga class? The algorithms and science behind social media pick up on your trends, your searches and views and will automatically send you posts and advertisements that coincide with these. It is as if Big Brother is truly watching – hello *1984*! George Orwell's prophetic book, written in 1948, describes a society in the future in, which all citizens are watched. It does make you feel like someone is watching when suddenly you see these ads for something that you were recently looking for pop up on your screen. But this is how the algorithm's work and they change. However, you cannot plan your post timing based on these or any assumptions that your content will automatically get shared to someone who was searching for it.

Finding your exact social media sweet spot is overrated. There is no such thing as the perfect time to post or the magic formula for the right combination of when and how many times to post. People check their social media posts all of the time so they will at some point see your posts. The key to success stems from focusing your content and posts on what is important for your audience, tailoring your message to truly what will impact your followers and spark that emotional response. So, no matter what time you choose to post, make sure your message is consistent, relevant and emotionally charged. The sweet spot will lie there right in your hands.

Myth 5:
My Product Doesn't Sell – Fix It with More Ads

My product isn't selling, it must be that I am not advertising it enough. I will fix it by placing more ads online. Really? Just because Facebook is telling you that you should Boost your post, doesn't mean that is the best way to go. It is no guarantee though that just because you spend the money to advertise that you will in fact reap any return on your investment at all.

It is very common for business owners, especially new entrepreneurs, to consider social media ad campaigns as the cure-all solution for selling a product or building a following. Many people believe that as long as we spend money on advertising, everything will work out just fine. I am not saying that paid advertising is not necessarily required. What I am saying is that it will not solve all of your problems or drive traffic to your website. It is by far a quick fix!

Let's look at a small non-profit organization looking to drive traffic to their website with the hope that people will see value in the services offered, the lives they impact and they will be moved to donate to the cause. The organization has a $1000 budget for the year for advertising expenses and they believe that their $1000 should convert to possibly thousands of dollars in donation revenue. Unfortunately for them, even with their good intentions, the ads have not driven the traffic to their website nor earned them any significant money in donations.

On its own, the non-profit's website does not convert followers to philanthropists so executives sought for a magic solution to their problem, thinking that social media ads were going to be their golden egg. Sadly, after spending too much money on ads, the organization received no donations at all.

Then there are of course those companies who do virtually no advertising, yet seem to come out on top. The fashion retailer, Zara, carefully studies their customers' desires and listens to what they want. Information is sent back to the design team daily, sharing what it is customers are looking for. This ingenious way of design development and producing what it is the customers want has inspired customers to share through word of mouth this incredible process. No advertising required!

Companies whose main objective is to meet a need will find that very little advertising is required. Each of the following companies followed several similar tactics in their marketing strategy instead of advertising and as you will see, they all have come out on top:

Costco, the second largest retailer in the world, does not do any advertising. By getting to know their customers first, they were able to achieve their success by customers sharing their amazing experiences in the store by word of mouth.

With products geared towards the adrenaline-junkie, GoPro established its presence in the market through its online videos, which depict other adventure seekers in action. The founders researched their target market and just knew that those who are on the constant search for the adrenaline rush would not be able to resist sharing the amazing stunts and feats that their fellow junkies had recorded. Thrill-seekers around the world shared information about the videos and camera products, building a community of others videotaping their own outdoor adventures. No advertising needed!

The award winning product produced by Tesla requires no fancy ads for you to know what it is. Executives at Tesla rely on the quality of their electric vehicle and the surge in environmental concern to propel the company's sales without spending a dollar on advertising. See for yourself how people talk after one of these high-tech, sleek vehicles passes them on the highway.

Word spreads like wildfire when someone has experienced excellent service, found a great product or feels important and respected. On the other hand, word of mouth can work against you as well. Have you ever had a poor experience at a restaurant and very quickly posted a negative review about your experience? People searching for a new restaurant read these reviews and they can weigh very heavily on someone's choice to dine there or not. As much as word of mouth is a good thing, it can also work against you if you have not ensured you meet all of the customers' requirements and needs.

The online retailer, Zappos, was built with word-of-mouth as their only marketing strategy. Spending their advertising budget instead on customer service, they have become one of the largest online retailers of clothing and shoes. Their strategy of excellent customer service has driven repeat business while word-of-mouth has continued to bring in new customers to experience it as well.

For each of these companies, there was, in fact, a formula to their success, which you can apply to your products and services as well. We will discuss in more detail in the next chapter how to use social media properly to help you attain the results you are looking for.

Part 2 - How to Use Social Media to Build Your Platform

In this day and age, if anyone ever thinks about social media marketing, one big platform comes to mind – Facebook. With the billions of users currently on that platform, it feels like the best place to market your offer, right? And if you think about it, the idea is quite sound. Think about the number of eyeballs your posts can get – and it is more likely that people will see you in a Facebook post rather than in a Google search. With today's use of social media, most people log onto Facebook every few minutes, scroll for a bit, laugh at a few memes – and in the meantime, see a few ads and posts. You don't see them going on Google for these things.

However, here's a thought: what if, one day, Facebook would cease to exist? One day, Mark Zuckerberg decided that he no longer wanted to go with Facebook. What if Facebook would slowly go into the background and become a distant memory?

Before you go and say that "that's not possible!" think about MySpace. Think about how popular it used to be before Facebook appeared. Every cool kid and every big business had a MySpace account – and aside from the people who did not know how to use a computer, everyone was connected on MySpace. A few years ago, if you wanted to become successful, you had to start with MySpace.

And there was a business at some point that did precisely that: they conducted all of their marketing moves on MySpace and became immensely popular. People were opting for their services, sharing their content – they were pretty much everywhere on the ads of MySpace. And that was precisely the problem: they were *only* on MySpace and no other platforms.

You can imagine that this was somewhat problematic when MySpace fell through, and the platform failed. A platform that was once so successful suddenly started losing all of its people – all of them migrating to Facebook, Instagram, and all the other "cool websites." The company in question lost all of its followers practically overnight – and they could never recover from the loss. This was simply because they no longer had the clients following them since they put all their faith in MySpace.

I don't want that to happen to you; therefore, I recommend viewing social media as a tool to build your platform. A platform that is yours, a platform you control, so you don't need to depend on the latest social media algorithmic changes or get someone else permission to get your message out there. You can build a platform in many ways, but I highly suggest providing an email list and using social media to grow that list. Email marketing is the number one best sales channel, and we are not going to stop using email anytime soon.

Plus, unlike Facebook and other social media platforms that filter who sees your content, email marketing will let everything go through. You control who sees the subject of your content. Once it goes into the inbox, it is all a matter of whether your follower opens your email or not.

The rest of this book will focus on how you can leverage social media to build a platform that you own. We will start with what to post on social media, move on with social media copywriting tips and end with how to do email marketing like a pro.

Chapter 6 - What and Where to Post on Social Media to Attract Your Target Audience

Your primary aim and ultimate goal with all your social media marketing efforts, regardless of which social media platform you use, should be to get people to sign up for your email list. Why? Because an email list is something that you own. It's yours. That's where the marketing magic is going to happen and you will turn those leads into raving fans and happy customers. I will talk more about email marketing in chapter 8, but first, let's look at where and what to post on social media to get those leads.

Post in Groups

The vast majority of social media interaction has moved away from the public feeds into closed groups. It's estimated that up to 80 percent of all social media chatter occurs in those groups. It doesn't matter if you are doing your marketing on Facebook, LinkedIn, or any other platform. Finding relevant and active groups in your niche is a must. These groups will quickly bring you to your target audience, mainly because most people in those groups share a common interest. Those groups can be pure gold and generate a flood of leads back to you and your business. The strategy for succeeding with group posting (and not being banned from the group) is simple. You slowly build up your authority within the group by posting valuable posts and comments, and step by step, drop more and more backlinks to your site and mention your service more regularly.

Posting on Instagram (feed/stories)

Instagram can be a massive lead generator if your strategy is right. Most people post endless feed-posts about their offers, making their feed look like an advertising page. Don't do that. Save your marketing efforts to your IG stories and treat your feed as a picture wall in your living room. When people visit your IG profile and glance at your feed posts, they should feel about you as a person or you as a company.

If you are using Instagram, make sure to optimize your profile page. Your profile headline is searchable on Google, so include some of your main niche keywords in there. And use the URL box and link back to your email sign-up page as well!

One last note on Instagram: treat Instagram as a tool to grow your business. That means that most of your "IG time" should be spent on creating content for your IG followers, not scrolling your feed.

Paid Social Media ads

I would not recommend paying for advertising if you are new to social media marketing. There are tons of ways to generate traffic for free. If you are more sophisticated and have a budget to spend, go ahead and try paid ads. The general strategy with paid ads, In my opinion, should be to get people to join your email list, but I might be wrong here. I'm not an expert in paid ads (yet), so I encourage you to do your research before starting your ad campaigns.

A note on giveaways

If you have been using Facebook or Instagram, you may have noticed that there are quite a few brands and pages that offer giveaways. "Share this post, tag a friend, and earn a chance to win something" is what most of these posts tend to say. These giveaways are not because the brands are oh-so-generous – it's because it's a good tactic to raise awareness for your brand and grow your following.

Even though this tactic might generate a flood of new followers, how many of them do you think care about you? I can give you a hint - not that many! Giveaways are a great way to get new followers, but most new followers are probably more interested in winning the giveaway than buying your offer. Be careful!

What to Post on Social Media?

We have touched on where to post; now, let's take some time and talk about *what* to post. There are hundreds of things that you may post on social media, all of which are directly related to your business. You need to decide which one works best at this point for your business. By making the right choice, you should increase your brand awareness and get more leads. Here are just a few of the countless ideas that you may post on social media.

- **Before and After Pictures**

Let's say that you are selling a product that would lead to a significant transformation. It may be a new hair dye, a face mask, a weight loss program, or even cabinet paint – whatever leads to a considerable change. To prove its effectiveness and get your leads, you may want to post before and after pictures that will showcase the effect of that product.

The transformation that you are showing may be personal, or it may be related to your business. For example, you may show before and after pictures of your website redesign. Or, if you are a nutritionist, you may post before and after photos of your customer's refrigerator – post-cleaning it. These small things are surely going to get potential customers interested.

- **Behind the Scenes Videos**

Followers are curious by nature, so a good thing to do would be to post behind-the-scenes videos. Share a few pictures of what's happening when working (try to catch the moments when you are going your hardest at it), and get your followers interested. Something good to post would be the location of a project, your office, or a special event that your company is hosting. This will allow customers to connect with you on a personal level.

- **How-to Posts**

How-to posts are also quite popular among followers. Here, you may share a blog post or a video showcasing how to do something specific – but that would also appeal to the ideal customer. Obviously, it should also appeal to your niche.

Let's say, for example, that your business is related to the wedding industry. In this case, you might want to make a post or a video on how to create decorations on a budget – or a photo booth for your wedding reception. You may opt for the help of other people that are skilled in the post creation – but if you use someone else's video, you might want to tag the creator of the video as well. This technique known as back linking might not only help them, but it might also bring clients from their page to yours.

- **Tips Articles**

Time-saving tips, money-saving tips, quick hacks – these types of posts are pretty popular among followers. For example, if you post promotional content about what you are selling, there is a chance that the followers will not click because they are not interested at that point. However, once they see post-market "tips," there's a part of their brain that will "activate" and make them curious.

You might think that giving them tips will not exactly help your product – but somewhere in the back of their minds, your followers will be influenced. For example, let's say that you are selling homemade cleaning solutions. In this case, an article on "tips to clean your house" might seem like it's just giving them general tips – but in truth, it will just make them more interested in cleaning products. This way, you are indirectly influencing them to buy your product.

- ### **What If I Don't Get Leads?**

If you aren't getting any leads, then it means that the tactic you are currently using is not effective. The campaign you are using might be poorly strategized, the budget might be wrong, or the campaign objective was not very well thought of. If you see that you aren't getting any leads, then you might want to ask yourself the following questions:

- ### **Am I giving value to my customers?**

You might think that you are selling a fantastic product that can change your customers' lives – but it might only change *your* life and be of no value to others. Think of the ideal customer, create a profile for them – and try to determine exactly who in your area might benefit from this product. You might want to create surveys to learn what the clients want and provide them valuable products.

- ### **Am I using the right metrics?**

If you aren't getting any leads, the chances are that your current event metrics are not exactly reliable. They may be focused more on the quantity of the contacts that came onto your page rather than on the quality (i.e., vanity metrics), and they are not telling you how many of those contacts are "bouncing." If the metrics are the problem, try shifting your focus to the ones based on the quality.

- **Am I posting the right content?**

Sometimes, the reason for you not getting any leads might be as simple as "your content is not interesting enough." It may be because you are not posting content to your customers' interest (content that might bring them informational value), or it might be that your content is simply boring, confusing, or poorly written. In this case, if the customer is not content with what you are posting, then it is pretty clear that you won't be generating any leads.

If this happens, there are two ways for you to go: first, you might want to try honing your copywriting skills. Learn a few tips and tricks (I show you how in chapter 8), and if you already have a way with words, this should be easy for you – with a little bit of practice. On the other hand, if you do not have the skills, you might want to hire someone with the necessary knowledge to give you this advantage. In most cases, just a few changes in your marketing campaign should be enough to get you the leads you need. Just figure out what went wrong, and try to correct each pressing matter.

Chapter 7 - How to Get Your Target Markets Attention on Social Media (crash course in copywriting)

Copywriting is the most undervalued skill in marketing. I don't know why, maybe because it's sexier to talk about ad spend and the hottest hashtags of the day? But let's be real here, getting good at copywriting can dramatically improve your overall marketing results and gets you more bang for every marketing unit (time, money, and energy) you invest.

Everything you write on social media is copywriting in one form or another—every single word. The text you include in your Instagram images is copywriting. The text you write in your caption is copywriting. The description on your Youtube video is copywriting. Everything you write is copywriting!

The reason for taking the time to learn how to master copywriting is simple. First, It will force you to look at the world from your audience's point of view. That act in itself is priceless in marketing. As we have talked about through this book, marketing is not about you or your company. Marketing is about *what's in it for your audience*. Why should they care? How will their lives be better? Copywriting pushes you to think about these questions and tailor your message, so it's crystal clear what's in it for them.

The classic copywriting formula AIDA

There are many different formulas for writing copy, and there are many different forms of copy. If you are writing a description for one of your products, that's copy. And if you are writing a Facebook ad for that product, that's copy as well. I highly recommend you take the time to learn the different types of copy you write in your business, but as a starting point, I recommend the classic copywriting formula AIDA. AIDA stands for attention, interest, desire, and action. You can think about AIDA as a general formula and adapt it to your specific needs.

Attention

Step number one is always to get people's attention. If you can't get their attention, well, it will be hard to accomplish anything. How do you get someone's attention on social media? It's not easy these days, but there are a few things you can do. First of all, you need to identify your target market. The words you use, the images you use, everything must be tailored to your target market. Using social media to get leads and customers is not about getting everyone's attention and "breaking through the noise," as we talked about earlier. It's getting the right people's attention. That's all that matters. When you design your images, don't think about what you think "looks good." Think instead about your target market. The same goes for headlines. Don't write "catchy" headlines for the sake of being catchy. Write headlines that resonate with your audience!

Interest/Desire

So you got your target market's attention, now what? Now it's time to start digging deeper, getting them to listen to what you have to say. This is the trickiest part. If you got their attention but didn't follow up with something interesting, they will most likely leave and never come back.

Let's say you write an attention-grabbing headline and get your ideal customer to start reading your post. What you need to do now to build up interest by sharing something they care about. You can do that by telling a story that resonates with them or talk about anything related to their hopes, fears, and dreams. The trick here is always to think, "what's in it for them? What's in it for them?" It's not about you at this stage; it's about them. It's about their interest, not yours.

When you nail the interest/desire part of your copy, your audience wants MORE. The copy you wrote has aroused them, got their blood pumping, and the dopamine flowing in their bodies. They want more, and they want it NOW.

Do you see how that works? You are not forcing them on anything at this point; you have grabbed their attention and built up their interest. You are almost there; all you need now is not to screw up the action part.

Action

You have probably heard of the term CTA before, which stands for *call to action*. CTAs are super important in copywriting. CTAs are what make people buy your stuff, sign up for your email list, reaching out to you, like your posts (not that important, but it's still an action), and telling their friends about how awesome you are.

A CTA is a prompt, statement, question at the end of your copy that works like an invisible hand that gets people to act on whatever you want them to act upon.

Here's the one thing that most people miss with a good CTA: you can never force someone to do something. An act must come from within; otherwise, it's manipulation. If you have done your job with getting their attention, making them interested in what you have to say, then the CTA doesn't need to be written in bold letters with tons of exclamation marks. All you need to do is to lead them wherever you want them to go.

Many people talk about CTA as if it's all that matters, but they are wrong. A CTA itself can rarely do all the heavy lifting. You as the marketer must get your prospects' attention, take them on a journey in your interest/desire phase and leave them with the decision of acting on your CTA. If you have done your job right, they will almost always act on the CTA. The key here (again) is to be authentic and know your audience, focusing on them and always ask yourself, "what's in it for them."

How to always have something to post

Coming up with new content is not that hard. When you are using the AIDA formula and focus on your target audience, you will get a TON of engagement on your posts. People will ask all kinds of questions, reach out to you to share their stories, and always provide you with new material. The trick to never run off of things to say is to listen to what your market is telling you, create a piece of content about that, and repeat the process.

One last note on copywriting

I have talked about the general frame you can use when writing your posts, ads, emails, and more. I have specifically not written his chapter with many plug-and-play templates simply because you have to develop your voice in your copy. The AIDA formula will get you here, even if it might require some experimentation.

Chapter 8. How to Use Social Media to Get Email Subscribers

How to get quality email subscribers

Step number one in getting started with email marketing (aside from the technical stuff) is to get people to sign up for your email list. That might sound simple, but it's not. An email list of people who want to hear from you is the most valuable asset any marketer can have. What makes it so valuable is the level of effort it takes for people to sign up in the first place. Most people hold on to their email addresses with all they got these days, asking questions: Is this valuable? Do I want his/her emails? What credentials do they have? The million-dollar question is always *how do I get more quality people to sign up for my list?!* Before I tell you how to do that, I will explain the differences between building an email list and providing an email list.

Building vs. providing an email list

You are probably familiar with the expression building an email list. I don't have anything against that; I'm a huge believer in email marketing. What I don't like is phrase *building*. I think a better way to view an email list is something you are *providing*. Let's discuss the difference.

When we talk about building an email list, it's easy to fall into the trap of the numbers game and only focus on getting as many subscribers as possible. Getting people to sign up for our list is essential, but not if they are the wrong type of people. When we talk about building an email list, we focus on the numbers of subscribers we have more than the quality of those subscribers.

On the other hand, when we phrase our email list as something we are providing, we automatically put our subscribers first, providing them with excellent content that makes their lives better. The providing mindset also forces us as marketers and creators to become more interesting people to have something interesting to share with our subscribers.

Viewing our email list as something we provide puts the focus on connecting with our subscribers. We discussed the same concept earlier in this book when we talked about the five social media marketing myths.

How do you get people to sign up for the list you are *providing*?

The key to getting people to consider joining your list is to give them something they want. How do you know what they want? You talk to them on social media. You engage with them, comment on their posts, DMing them, answering their questions, and consistently scanning your market for new insights. If you do that, you will develop a nose for knowing what your target audience cares for, allowing you to produce a so-called "lead magnet" you can give them in exchange for their email address. If your lead magnet is good, which means it contains better stuff than people can find for free on Wikipedia, and you also *overdeliver* on their expectations, you are on your way to success.

What to send your subscribers, and how often to send it

If it's challenging to get people to join your list, the actual email marketing game begins after they have signed up. When people first sign up, they will typically get your lead magnet and a few pre-written emails (often called a welcome sequence) delivered in the next 1-2 weeks so they can get to know you and your world better. If they like what they get, they will stay on your list, and if they don't, they will unsubscribe (which is fine). After they have finished the welcome sequence, it's your job as the creator to keep serving them with excellent content regularly. I have talked about content creating and copywriting earlier in this book, and it's the same strategies that apply here. Listen to what they say, and always ask yourselves *What's in it for them?*

There are no "rules" of how often you should email your list. Sometimes I send two emails per week, and sometimes I send two per month to my lists. How frequently you send emails to your list is your decision, but a minimum is probably once a month after they have gotten to know you. The more important question is: *do you have something interesting to say that will benefit your subscribers?* If the answer to that question is no, you should probably not send anything.

On the other hand, if the answer is *hell yeah!* - go ahead and send those emails asap! What you are trying to accomplish is to create a bond with your subscribers. You want them to know that the emails you send are interesting and packed with value. You want them to open, read and share your message on your behalf.

Approaching your list like that will push you to find exciting articles/ideas and package that in a way that can benefit your subscribers. And in that process, what you are doing is not just marketing; you make people's lives better. When you reach that point, selling your product/service feels like an obligation.

How to sell in email

Think about all the sales emails you have received over the years. Now think about the last time you bought something from an email. Why did you do that? Probably because you trusted that person, they offered you something you wanted, gave you a reason to buy, and induced a little scarcity.

Selling your product/service in email is as simple as putting in front of the right people, giving them a reason to buy and then leaving the decision up to them, as we talked about in the copywriting section of this book.

If you followed the steps I've discussed in this chapter, you would use social media to get quality email subscribers and slowly build relationships with them. They trust you. They know you have exciting things to say, so selling your product/service will feel natural.

Conclusion

Social media is an excellent, powerful tool that can transform your business into a thriving, well-oiled machine if you use it strategically to your advantage. I hope that through this book, I have provided you with information and things that you should avoid doing as well as those that you should do to succeed. Keep in mind that your goal is to provide compelling content, connect with people, and establish a relationship. Instead of hunting for likes, tricking into clicking methods, you want to create these relationships through your ability to provide them with what they need and express it so that each person feels heard and feels an emotional connection.

Start by avoiding the myths and use the tools, skills, and strategies that you have on hand to make your email list grow. Because after all, you may have many people following your page – but unless you own your platform and control if they see your message or not, it might all be for nothing.

Connect With the Author

Hey,

There are plenty of great marketing books online, so thank you for choosing *Likes Don't Pay Bills* and reading all the way to the end!

What I hate after reading a book is the feeling that it's stuffed with bad and boring content that's easily found for free online. If I gave you that, let me know in the reviews. On the other hand, If I gave you what you expected (or more), please tell me that in the reviews as well!

This book results from years of trial and error blended with online courses, reading countless marketing books, and talking to smart people about marketing. I hope I have given you something worth your time, despite not being a native English writer.

I'm from Sweden, where I live and work. I spend a good amount of my time coaching people in building online businesses.

If you want to connect with me, learn all about Swedish Fika, and get my monthly marketing email Swedish Fika and Marketing Strategies, go to christianoberg.com/strategies

Regards,

Christian Oberg
christianoberg.com

www.ingramcontent.com/pod-product-compliance
Lightning Source LLC
Chambersburg PA
CBHW072135150726
48002CB00004B/1519